BILLIE EILISH BIOGRAPHY STORY FOR KIDS:
FROM FAMILY SONGS TO GRAMMY WINS

LUIS B. MERCER

BILLIE EILISH…………..

Copyright ©2024 All rights reserved by Luis B. Mercer.

No part of this publication may be reproduced or transmitted in any form or by any means including photocopying, recording or other electronic or mechanical methods without the prior written permission of the publisher except in the case of brief quotations embodied in critical reviews and certain other non-commercial uses- permitted by copyright

BILLIE EILISH..............

Table of contents

Introduction........................5

Chapter 1: A Star is Born: Meet Billie Eilish...........................7

Chapter 2: A Creative Family: Growing Up with Music................................12

Chapter 3: Writing Her First Song: The Start of Something Special....................................18

Chapter 4: The Bedroom Studio: Where It All Began..24

Chapter 5: Ocean Eyes: The Song That Changed Everything.....................................30

Chapter 6: The Journey to Stardom: Hard Work and Big Dreams..37

Chapter 7: Billie's Unique Style: Standing Out in a Crowd......................................44

Chapter 8: Making an Album: When We All Fall Asleep, Where Do We Go?..............................50

Chapter 9: Winning Big: Billie's Grammy Night...58

Chapter 10: Inspiring the World: More Than Just Music...66

Chapter 11: Billie's Biggest Fans: Connecting with Kids Like You...74

Chapter 13: Lessons from Billie: Dare to Be Different.....................................89

Chapter 14: A Legacy of Inspiration and Empowerment..........................97

Fun facts about Billie Eilish..106

Trivia questions........................112

Conclusion..............................131

BILLIE EILISH..............

Introduction Meet Billie Eilish, the pop star who's as unique as her music! From a young age, Billie stood out with her striking green hair, oversized clothes, and a voice that can make you laugh, cry, and think all at once. Born in Los Angeles in 2001, she was raised in a creative family that loved music just as much as she did. But Billie wasn't like the other kids—she didn't just want to sing; she wanted to change the way we listen to music. With her hauntingly beautiful melodies and thought-provoking lyrics, Billie's songs are like stories set to music. She's not afraid to speak her mind and tackle big topics like mental health, identity, and growing up in today's world. From her breakout hit "Ocean Eyes" to winning Grammy Awards, Billie's journey is one of creativity, courage, and staying true to

BILLIE EILISH…………..

herself. Get ready to dive into the world of Billie Eilish—a world where music, style, and big dreams come together to inspire kids like you to dream big and be unapologetically yourself!

Chapter 1: A Star is Born: Meet Billie Eilish

Billie Eilish Pirate Baird O'Connell was born on December 18, 2001, in Los Angeles, California. From the very beginning, Billie was no ordinary child. She grew up in a cozy, creative neighborhood called Highland Park, surrounded by music, art, and endless possibilities. Her parents, Maggie Baird and Patrick O'Connell, were artists themselves. Maggie was an actress and screenwriter, while Patrick worked in the entertainment industry too. It seemed like creativity ran in the family!

Even as a baby, Billie had a spark that caught everyone's attention. She had bright blue eyes, a mischievous grin, and an undeniable sense of curiosity. Billie loved exploring her surroundings and found joy in everything, whether it was a piece of paper she could scribble on or a song her mom would hum.

Billie didn't grow up in a mansion or with the luxuries you might imagine a future superstar would have. Her family wasn't rich, but they were rich in love, talent, and creativity. Maggie and Patrick believed in raising their children with lots of freedom to dream and express themselves. They homeschooled Billie and her older brother, Finneas O'Connell, giving them plenty of time to explore their interests.

Growing up, Billie wasn't just interested in music. She loved dancing, acting, and even crafting. But music held a special place in her heart. Billie's parents often played old records and shared songs by bands like The Beatles and artists like Frank Sinatra. Little

BILLIE EILISH..............

Billie listened carefully, tapping her feet to the rhythm and singing along with her sweet, childlike voice.

One of Billie's favorite activities as a toddler was banging on pots and pans in the kitchen. She'd turn the kitchen floor into her personal drum set, making up beats and laughing as her family cheered her on. It was clear from a young age that Billie was destined to create music.

Billie was also very imaginative. She loved creating stories in her head and turning them into songs, even if they were about simple things like her dog, Pepper, or the flowers in her backyard. Her creativity wasn't just limited to music—Billie would also design her outfits and dream about being on stage, even though she was still too young to know what her future would hold.

BILLIE EILISH..............

Despite her cheerful and playful nature, Billie faced challenges as a child. She was diagnosed with Tourette Syndrome, a condition that made her body twitch or move in ways she couldn't control. Some kids might have found this hard to deal with, but Billie's family supported her, reminding her that her uniqueness was her strength. This made Billie even more determined to embrace who she was.

Her childhood was filled with little moments that planted the seeds for her incredible journey. Whether it was singing in the car with her mom, watching her dad play the piano, or writing short poems with her brother, Billie's world revolved around creativity and connection.

Through it all, Billie remained a dreamer. She loved imagining a world where her music would inspire people. Little did she know, she would soon become one of the most famous and beloved artists in the world, touching hearts with her voice and her story.

Chapter 2: A Creative Family: Growing Up with Music

Billie Eilish's journey to stardom started with the people closest to her: her family. In the O'Connell household, creativity wasn't just encouraged—it was a way of life. Billie's parents, Maggie Baird and Patrick O'Connell, were both artists who valued the power of self-expression. They created an environment where imagination, music, and storytelling flourished.

Maggie, an actress and musician, often filled the house with songs. She played the piano and guitar and encouraged Billie and her brother Finneas to do the same. Maggie also wrote songs, and sometimes, Billie and Finneas would join in, making music together as a family. Patrick, a construction worker and part-time actor, brought a love of performing and storytelling to their lives. He would share fascinating tales from his acting experiences, sparking young Billie's imagination.

Billie's older brother, Finneas O'Connell, was another key figure in her creative journey. Finneas had a knack for music from an early age. He learned to play multiple instruments, wrote songs, and had a small studio setup in his bedroom. Billie looked up to Finneas and often followed him around, soaking up everything he knew about music and production. Finneas wasn't just a big brother—he was a mentor, collaborator, and lifelong best friend.

The O'Connells lived modestly in their Los Angeles home. They didn't have flashy cars or luxurious vacations, but they had something far more valuable: time together. Since Billie and Finneas were homeschooled, they spent most of their days exploring their interests. Maggie, as their teacher, designed lessons that sparked their curiosity. One day they might study poetry, and the next, they'd dive into music theory or film projects.

Music was always present in their home. The family would gather to listen to artists like The Beatles, Green Day, and Billie Holiday. Maggie introduced Billie to timeless classics, while Finneas introduced her to modern pop and alternative music. This blend of old and new shaped Billie's unique sound.

Another big part of Billie's creative upbringing was freedom. Her parents believed in letting their kids express themselves in any way they wanted. If Billie wanted to wear mismatched clothes or dye her hair an unusual color, they encouraged her. This freedom gave Billie the confidence to embrace her individuality, something that would later become a hallmark of her identity as an artist.

Even though Billie was naturally talented, her family taught her the importance of hard work and resilience. Maggie and Patrick often reminded their children that success wasn't just about talent—it was about dedication, practice, and staying true to oneself. This lesson stuck with Billie as she began to explore her passion for music more seriously.

Family time often included creative experiments. Maggie and Patrick would ask

Billie and Finneas to write short stories or poems, which they would then turn into songs. Sometimes, these experiments were just for fun, but other times, they sparked real ideas. Billie quickly discovered she had a talent for songwriting, weaving her emotions and thoughts into melodies.

One of the most magical things about Billie's family was how they supported each other's dreams. When Finneas started recording songs in his bedroom studio, Billie would eagerly join him. At first, she was shy, but with Finneas's encouragement, she began to sing more confidently. Little did they know that this sibling collaboration would one day lead to worldwide hits.

The O'Connells weren't just a family; they were a team. Each member played a role in nurturing Billie's creativity. Her parents provided guidance and inspiration, and her brother became her biggest collaborator. Together, they built a foundation of love, trust, and creativity that would shape Billie's journey as an artist.

As Billie grew older, her family's influence became even more apparent. The lessons they taught her—about hard work, embracing individuality, and staying connected to her roots—remained with her throughout her rise to fame. No matter how big her dreams became, Billie always remembered where she came from and the family who believed in her every step of the way.

Chapter 3: Writing Her First Song: The Start of Something Special

Billie Eilish's first steps into songwriting were like opening the door to a magical new world. She had always loved music, but turning her own thoughts and feelings into songs was something entirely different. It was exciting, personal, and a little scary. Luckily, Billie had the perfect guide—her older brother, Finneas O'Connell.

Billie's first song came to life when she was just 11 years old. It wasn't a planned event; it was more like a happy accident. One day, during a family songwriting session led by their mom, Maggie, Billie and Finneas started brainstorming ideas. Maggie often encouraged them to write songs based on their feelings or experiences, no matter how small or big they seemed.

For Billie, this was a chance to express herself. She had always been full of emotions and stories, and songwriting gave her a way to let them out. With Finneas helping her shape the melody and lyrics, Billie wrote her very first song, titled "Fingers Crossed."

"Fingers Crossed" was inspired by one of Billie's favorite TV shows at the time—The Walking Dead. She imagined what it might feel like to survive in a post-apocalyptic world, running from zombies and fighting for survival. The song was haunting, emotional, and deeply imaginative, just like Billie herself.

As Billie sang the lyrics for the first time, her family was amazed. She had a voice that could tell a story, full of raw emotion and depth. Finneas, who had already been working on his own music, was especially impressed. He encouraged Billie to keep writing and promised to help her record her songs.

For Billie, writing that first song felt magical. It was like she had unlocked a hidden talent she didn't even know she had. The process of putting her thoughts and feelings into words and melodies was freeing. It allowed her to explore her emotions and connect with the world in a new way.

From that moment on, Billie began writing songs more often. She would sit in her room with a notebook and jot down lyrics whenever inspiration struck. Sometimes her songs were about imaginary stories, like "Fingers Crossed," and other times they were deeply personal. Billie wasn't afraid to explore her feelings, whether it was happiness, sadness, or something in between.

Finneas became her biggest supporter and collaborator. With his growing skills in music production, he helped Billie record her songs in their tiny bedroom studio. They didn't have fancy equipment, but they made the most of what they had. Finneas would play the guitar or piano, while Billie sang her heart out.

One of the most important things Billie learned during this time was that songwriting wasn't about being perfect. It was about being honest. She realized that the best songs came from real emotions, even if they were messy or complicated. This belief would later become the foundation of her music career.

Writing her first song was also a turning point for Billie in another way—it gave her a sense of purpose. She realized that music wasn't just something she loved; it was something she wanted to do forever. It was a way to express herself, connect with others, and make sense of the world around her.

As Billie continued to write and record songs, her confidence grew. She started experimenting with different styles and sounds, often blending elements of pop, alternative, and even electronic music. Her creativity knew no bounds, and she wasn't afraid to take risks.

BILLIE EILISH…………..

Looking back, "Fingers Crossed" was just the beginning. It was the first spark of a musical journey that would one day captivate millions of fans around the world. For Billie, it was proof that her voice—and her story—mattered.

That first song wasn't just a milestone; it was a promise to herself. A promise to keep dreaming, creating, and sharing her heart with the world, one song at a time.

Chapter 4: The Bedroom Studio: Where It All Began

Billie Eilish's rise to stardom didn't start in a massive recording studio with expensive equipment and a team of producers.
Instead, it began in a small, cozy bedroom in her family's Los Angeles home. This was the place where Billie and her older brother, Finneas, turned their shared love of music into something extraordinary.
The bedroom studio was Finneas's domain. It wasn't fancy—just a simple setup with a computer, a microphone, and a few instruments. But what it lacked in equipment, it made up for in creativity. Finneas loved experimenting with sounds, layering melodies, and figuring out how to produce music on his own. He had already

been writing and recording his own songs, but when Billie joined him, something magical happened.

At first, Billie was a little shy about singing in front of her brother. She admired Finneas's talent and worried that her voice wouldn't measure up. But Finneas believed in Billie and encouraged her to sing with confidence. He often told her, "Your voice is special. People need to hear it." Those words stuck with Billie and gave her the courage to let her voice shine.

The first big project they worked on together in the bedroom studio was a song called "Ocean Eyes." Billie's dance teacher had asked her to create a song for a choreography piece, and she turned to Finneas for help. He had written "Ocean Eyes" earlier but hadn't recorded it yet.

When Billie sang the song for the first time, it was as if it was meant to be hers. Her voice brought the lyrics to life in a way that felt emotional and pure.

Recording "Ocean Eyes" in the bedroom studio was a simple but exciting process. Finneas played the instruments and managed the production, while Billie stood in front of the microphone, pouring her heart into every note. They recorded multiple takes until they found the perfect version. The entire process felt natural and fun, like two siblings hanging out and doing what they loved.

When they finished the song, neither of them expected much to happen. They uploaded it to a platform called SoundCloud, where people could listen to and share music for free. It was a casual decision—just a way to share the song with Billie's dance teacher and a few friends.

But something incredible happened. Within days, "Ocean Eyes" started gaining attention. People from all over the world were listening to the song and sharing it online. Listeners were captivated by Billie's unique voice and the haunting beauty of the song. Suddenly, the bedroom studio didn't seem so small anymore.

The success of "Ocean Eyes" was a turning point for Billie and Finneas. It showed them that their music had the power to reach people far beyond their little corner of Los Angeles. The bedroom studio became their creative haven, a place where they could dream big and experiment freely.

Over time, Billie and Finneas created more songs in that same space. They worked late into the night, bouncing ideas off each other and pushing each other to be better. Their partnership was built on trust, respect, and a shared love of music. They weren't just siblings—they were a team.

The bedroom studio became the birthplace of Billie's first album, "When We All Fall Asleep, Where Do We Go?" Finneas handled the production while Billie brought her raw emotions and unique perspective to the lyrics and melodies. Together, they crafted a sound that was fresh, honest, and completely their own.

Even as Billie's career took off, she never forgot the bedroom studio where it all began. It was a reminder of her roots, her family, and the magic of creating something out of nothing.

BILLIE EILISH…………..

The story of the bedroom studio is proof that you don't need fancy equipment or a big budget to make great art. All you need is passion, creativity, and the courage to follow your dreams. For Billie and Finneas, that little room wasn't just a studio—it was the start of a musical revolution.

Chapter 5: Ocean Eyes: The Song That Changed Everything

Sometimes, a single moment can change your entire life. For Billie Eilish, that moment came with a song called "Ocean Eyes." What started as a simple recording project for her dance teacher quickly became the song that introduced Billie to the world—and nothing was ever the same again.

The story of "Ocean Eyes" begins in Billie's early teen years. She was taking dance classes and loved expressing herself through movement. One day, her dance teacher asked if Billie could bring in a song for a choreography project. Billie turned to her brother, Finneas, for help.

Finneas had written "Ocean Eyes" earlier and thought it would be a perfect fit for Billie's voice. The song was delicate and emotional, with lyrics that spoke of longing and heartbreak. It felt personal, even though Billie hadn't written it herself.

When Billie first sang "Ocean Eyes," something magical happened. Her voice, soft yet powerful, brought the song to life in a way that no one could have expected. It was as if the song was meant for her all along.

Recording the Song

In their small bedroom studio, Billie and Finneas worked together to record "Ocean Eyes." Billie stood in front of the microphone, letting the words and melodies flow naturally. Finneas handled the production, adding layers of sound that complemented Billie's voice.

The recording process was simple and fun. Billie loved the experience of creating something beautiful with her brother. Neither of them could have imagined what would happen next.

Sharing the Song

After they finished the recording, Billie and Finneas uploaded "Ocean Eyes" to SoundCloud, a platform where people could share and discover music. The main goal was to let Billie's dance teacher hear it, but they also hoped a few friends might listen. To their surprise, the song didn't just reach their friends—it started spreading like wildfire. Listeners from all over the world discovered "Ocean Eyes" and fell in love with Billie's unique voice and the haunting beauty of the song. Within days, the track had thousands of plays.

The Viral Moment

As "Ocean Eyes" gained popularity, music blogs and social media users began sharing it. People were curious about the mysterious young artist behind the song. Billie's voice sounded so mature and emotional, yet she was just a teenager recording music in her brother's bedroom.

The buzz around "Ocean Eyes" caught the attention of music industry professionals. Soon, Billie and Finneas were receiving messages from record labels, producers, and managers who wanted to work with them. It was an overwhelming experience, but Billie stayed grounded, thanks to her supportive family.

A Star Is Born

"Ocean Eyes" became Billie's first big break. It was more than just a song—it was her introduction to the world as an artist. People were drawn to her honesty, her unique sound, and the emotion she poured into every note.

For Billie, the success of "Ocean Eyes" was both exciting and surreal. She never expected a song she recorded for fun would turn her into a rising star. It was a dream come true, but it also came with challenges. Suddenly, Billie's life was changing in ways she couldn't have imagined.

The Meaning Behind the Song

BILLIE EILISH…………..

Even though Finneas wrote "Ocean Eyes," Billie made it her own. The song's lyrics, about vulnerability and deep emotions, resonated with listeners of all ages. It was the kind of song that made people feel something, and that was exactly what Billie wanted her music to do.

Years later, Billie still credits "Ocean Eyes" as the song that started it all. It opened doors she never thought possible and set the stage for her incredible career. But more importantly, it showed her that music could connect people in powerful ways.

The success of "Ocean Eyes" taught Billie an important lesson: Sometimes, the most unexpected moments can lead to the greatest opportunities. All it takes is a little

BILLIE EILISH…………..

courage, a lot of passion, and the willingness to share your voice with the world.

Chapter 6: The Journey to Stardom: Hard Work and Big Dreams

After the success of "Ocean Eyes," Billie Eilish's life changed overnight. She went from a teenager recording music in her bedroom to an artist recognized around the world. But this wasn't the end of her story—it was just the beginning. Billie's journey to stardom was full of challenges, hard work, and unwavering dedication to her dreams.

The attention from "Ocean Eyes" brought Billie into the public eye, but it also meant she needed to decide what kind of artist she wanted to be. Billie wasn't interested in following trends or copying other musicians. She wanted to be authentic, expressing herself in a way that felt true to who she was.

With the help of her brother, Finneas, Billie started writing and recording more songs. They experimented with different sounds, blending dreamy melodies with emotional lyrics. The siblings shared a creative bond that allowed them to push boundaries and create music that stood out.

One of their early releases, "Bellyache," showcased Billie's unique ability to tell stories through her music. The song was quirky, dark, and unlike anything else at the time. It was clear that Billie wasn't just a singer—she was a storyteller with a bold vision.

As Billie released more music, her fanbase began to grow. She connected with listeners through platforms like SoundCloud, YouTube, and social media. Fans loved her raw honesty, her distinct style, and her willingness to talk about difficult emotions. Billie's rise was also fueled by live performances. Despite her young age, she had a natural presence on stage. Her concerts felt intimate, almost like she was singing directly to each person in the audience. Fans appreciated how real and approachable she seemed, both on and off stage.

Balancing Life and Fame
As Billie's career took off, she faced the challenge of balancing her new life as a star with her everyday life as a teenager. She was still attending school, spending time with

her family, and navigating the ups and downs of growing up.

Fame brought exciting opportunities but also new pressures. Billie had to learn how to handle interviews, photo shoots, and public appearances while staying true to herself. It wasn't always easy, but her strong support system—especially her family—helped her stay grounded.

The Role of Hard Work

Behind the scenes, Billie and Finneas were working harder than ever. They spent countless hours in their makeshift studio, writing and recording songs. Every detail mattered, from the lyrics to the production, and they wanted everything to be perfect. Billie also started working with a management team to plan her career. They helped her navigate the music industry, book shows, and promote her music. But even with professional support, Billie remained hands-on in every aspect of her career. She wanted her music and image to reflect her personality and vision.

Staying True to Her Dreams
Throughout her journey, Billie stayed focused on her dreams. She wanted to create music that made people feel something, whether it was joy, sadness, or inspiration. She also wanted to break stereotypes about what a pop star should look or sound like. Billie's boldness and creativity paid off. Her music began charting internationally, and she started receiving invitations to perform at major festivals and events. But through it all, she remained humble and grateful,

always remembering the little bedroom studio where it all began.

Inspiring Others

Billie's story inspired many young people to pursue their passions. She proved that you don't have to fit into a mold to succeed. Her journey showed that being different isn't just okay—it can be your greatest strength. As Billie worked toward her first album, she knew she was on the brink of something incredible. But she also understood that true success wasn't just about fame or awards. For her, it was about staying true to her art and connecting with her fans in meaningful ways.

Billie's big dream was simple: to make music that mattered. She didn't want to be just another artist on the radio. She wanted to leave a lasting impact, inspiring people to embrace their emotions, their uniqueness, and their creativity.

This journey to stardom was just the beginning of Billie's story. There were still many milestones ahead, but she was ready to face them with determination and heart.

Chapter 7: Billie's Unique Style: Standing Out in a Crowd

Billie Eilish is known for more than just her music—she's also famous for her unique style. From oversized clothes to brightly colored hair, Billie's look is as bold and creative as her songs. But her style isn't just about making a statement. It's a reflection of her personality, her values, and her desire to be true to herself.

Dressing Differently
When Billie started gaining fame, people noticed right away that she didn't dress like other pop stars. Instead of wearing glamorous dresses or tight-fitting outfits, Billie chose baggy clothes that hid her body shape.

Why did she dress this way? Billie wanted people to focus on her music and not judge her based on how she looked. She also wanted to challenge the idea that female artists had to dress a certain way to be successful. Her outfits sent a powerful message: It's okay to be different.
Billie's style became her trademark. She often wore brightly colored tracksuits, oversized hoodies, and sneakers. She loved mixing bold patterns and textures, creating looks that were fun and unpredictable. Her outfits showed that she wasn't afraid to take risks or stand out from the crowd.

Expressing Herself Through Fashion
For Billie, fashion is a way to express her mood and creativity. She sees clothing as another form of art, just like music. Her

outfits often reflect her personality—bold, edgy, and a little mysterious.

One of Billie's favorite things about fashion is how it allows her to experiment. She loves trying new styles and pushing boundaries. Whether she's wearing neon green or head-to-toe black, Billie's looks always make a statement.

Hair That Makes Headlines

Billie's hair is another part of her unique style. Over the years, she's dyed her hair nearly every color you can imagine—blue, green, silver, black, and even neon yellow. Each new hairstyle became a trend, inspiring fans around the world to copy her look.

Her bold hair choices show that Billie isn't afraid to take risks. She loves surprising people and keeping them guessing about what she'll do next. For Billie, her hair is just another way to express herself and have fun.

The Meaning Behind the Clothes
While Billie's outfits are fun and eye-catching, they also carry a deeper meaning. Billie has spoken openly about how she wants to feel comfortable in her own skin without worrying about what others think.
She's also used her style to challenge beauty standards and stereotypes. By wearing clothes that cover her body, Billie sends a powerful message: People shouldn't be judged by their appearance. She wants her fans to know that it's okay to dress however they like, as long as it makes them happy.

BILLIE EILISH..............

As Billie became more famous, her style caught the attention of the fashion world. She's worked with top designers and even created her own clothing lines. Despite her success, Billie has stayed true to her unique look. She still loves oversized clothes, bold colors, and anything that feels authentically "her."

Her influence on fashion has been huge. Many young people admire Billie not just for her music, but for her confidence and individuality. She's inspired a whole generation to embrace their personal style and not worry about fitting in.

Billie's approach to fashion is all about breaking the rules. She doesn't follow trends or try to fit in with what's popular. Instead, she creates her own trends and encourages others to do the same.

BILLIE EILISH…………..

Her willingness to be different has made her a role model for kids and teenagers around the world. Billie shows that it's okay to be yourself, even if you don't look or act like everyone else.

Why It Matters
Billie's unique style isn't just about clothes—it's about confidence, creativity, and self-expression. By staying true to herself, Billie has shown that being different can be a strength. Her style has become a symbol of her fearless attitude and her commitment to inspiring others.

Chapter 8: Making an Album: When We All Fall Asleep, Where Do We Go?

Billie Eilish's first album, When We All Fall Asleep, Where Do We Go?, was released in 2019 and marked a turning point in her career. This album wasn't just a collection of songs—it was a deeply personal, genre-bending work that showcased Billie's growth as an artist and her willingness to explore new sounds and ideas. It was a window into her mind, her fears, her dreams, and her deepest thoughts.

The Vision Behind the Album
Billie's vision for When We All Fall Asleep, Where Do We Go? was clear from the start. She wanted to create an album that was dark, mysterious, and a little bit scary. The

title reflected the album's theme of sleep and dreams—a place where strange, magical things can happen. Billie wanted listeners to feel like they were stepping into a dream world, where reality and fantasy blur.
With Finneas at her side, Billie spent months writing and recording songs that explored themes of fear, anxiety, and vulnerability. They created a soundscape that was haunting and atmospheric, blending elements of pop, electronic, and even some rock influences. The result was an album that was both unexpected and unforgettable.
Creating the album was a labor of love. Billie and Finneas worked tirelessly in their bedroom studio, fine-tuning every detail. They experimented with different sounds, recorded hundreds of takes, and spent hours

listening to mixes. The process was all-consuming, but it was also incredibly rewarding.

One of the standout tracks from the album was "bad guy," a song that perfectly captured Billie's quirky, dark sense of humor. The song was infectious, with a beat that was impossible to resist. It was also a little cheeky, with lyrics that poked fun at traditional ideas of masculinity.

Billie's writing style was raw and honest, tackling subjects like mental health, teenage angst, and self-doubt. Her lyrics were poetic, sometimes cryptic, but always sincere. She wasn't afraid to be vulnerable or to question everything. For Billie, this album was about breaking the rules and exploring uncharted territory.

BILLIE EILISH…………..

Collaborations and Contributions

When We All Fall Asleep, Where Do We Go? wasn't just a solo effort. Billie collaborated with a variety of talented musicians, producers, and artists who helped bring her vision to life. She worked with people who understood her sound and who were willing to take risks alongside her.

One of the most memorable collaborations was with Justin Bieber on the track "bad guy (Remix)," which introduced Billie's music to a wider audience. The song topped charts around the world and brought Billie international recognition. It was a testament to her hard work and creativity that she was able to blend genres and reach new fans.

The Impact of the Album

BILLIE EILISH..............

When We All Fall Asleep, Where Do We Go? became an instant hit, debuting at number one on the Billboard 200 chart. It received critical acclaim and won several Grammy Awards, including Album of the Year. Billie became the youngest artist ever to win this prestigious award, solidifying her place in music history.

The album's success was a triumph for Billie and Finneas, but it also represented something larger. It showed that young people were hungry for something new and different. They wanted music that spoke to them, that reflected their own struggles and fears. Billie's album provided that—and more.

After the album's release, Billie and Finneas embarked on a world tour to promote it. They performed songs from When We All

Fall Asleep, Where Do We Go? to sold-out crowds, giving fans a glimpse into Billie's mind and her creative process. The concerts were an experience—immersive, emotional, and unforgettable.

Billie's tour wasn't just about performing music—it was about creating a connection with her fans. She wanted her audience to leave the concert feeling inspired, feeling less alone in their struggles. Billie's performances were a mix of art, storytelling, and raw emotion. They showed her vulnerability and her strength.

Beyond the Music

The success of When We All Fall Asleep, Where Do We Go? wasn't just about the music—it was about the message behind it. Billie used her platform to speak out about mental health, environmental issues, and the importance of being true to oneself. She became an advocate for change, using her music and her voice to make a difference. Billie's album was a catalyst for conversations about the darker side of fame, the pressures of perfection, and the reality of growing up in a social media world. She encouraged her fans to question everything and to be authentic, even if it meant going against the grain.

The Future Ahead
With the success of When We All Fall Asleep, Where Do We Go? behind her, Billie Eilish was poised for even greater things. She had proven herself as a trailblazer, a voice for a new generation, and an artist who wasn't afraid to push boundaries.

Billie's future was bright, and she was ready to continue her journey with confidence and excitement.

Her dreams for the future were ambitious. Billie wanted to keep making music that mattered, to experiment with new sounds, and to keep evolving as an artist. She also hoped to use her platform to inspire others, to remind them that they could chase their dreams, no matter how big or small.

When We All Fall Asleep, Where Do We Go? was just the beginning. There was still so much more to come from Billie Eilish.

Chapter 9: Winning Big: Billie's Grammy Night

Billie Eilish's Grammy Night was an unforgettable moment in music history. It wasn't just about winning awards—it was about breaking records, making history, and solidifying her place as one of the most influential young artists of her generation. The night was a celebration of hard work, creativity, and the power of following your dreams.

A Historic Moment
The 2020 Grammy Awards will always be remembered as the night Billie Eilish made history. At just 18 years old, Billie became the youngest artist ever to win the prestigious Album of the Year award for

When We All Fall Asleep, Where Do We Go? She also took home trophies for Best New Artist, Best Pop Vocal Album, and Best Engineered Album, Non-Classical.

For Billie, the Grammys were a dream come true. She had always been a fan of music's biggest night, watching with her family and imagining what it would be like to stand on that stage, holding a Grammy in her hand. Now, she was living that dream.

Preparing for the Big Night

Leading up to the Grammy Awards, Billie was a bundle of nerves and excitement. The pressure was on—she was nominated in multiple categories and had a strong chance of winning. Billie, Finneas, and the team spent weeks preparing her performances, making sure everything was perfect. They rehearsed tirelessly, refining every detail, from the staging to the lighting to the wardrobe.

Billie's outfit for the night was another statement—a custom Gucci suit with oversized sleeves that concealed her hands. It was a nod to her love for unconventional fashion, and it was part of her plan to surprise and captivate the audience. Billie was known for her unique style, and she wanted her Grammy night look to reflect that.

Performances that Stood Out
On the night of the Grammy Awards, Billie Eilish took the stage for a performance that left an indelible mark. She started with "bad guy," the song that had become her breakout hit. The audience sang along to every word,

their energy and excitement feeding into Billie's performance. The song's catchy beat and edgy lyrics were a perfect introduction to Billie's style—raw, unapologetic, and unforgettable.

Following "bad guy," Billie performed "When the Party's Over," a haunting ballad about sadness and the end of something beautiful. The song showcased Billie's ability to convey complex emotions through music, and it resonated deeply with the audience. Her voice was powerful, yet fragile—honest and vulnerable.

Billie's performances were a masterclass in emotion and storytelling. She didn't just sing the songs—she brought them to life. She used her voice, her body language, and her presence to create an experience that was as moving as it was memorable.

BILLIE EILISH..............

The Moment of Truth

As the night wore on, the tension built. Billie was up for several awards, and the competition was fierce. When it came time for the Album of the Year announcement, the room fell silent. The envelope was opened, and the name inside was clear: Billie Eilish.

Billie's reaction was one of pure disbelief and joy. She burst into tears as she walked to the stage, hugged her brother Finneas, and accepted the award. It was a moment she had dreamed of for years, and now it was real. Billie's family, friends, and fans were watching, and they were just as thrilled as she was.

Holding the Grammy in her hand, Billie gave a short, heartfelt speech. She thanked her family, her team, her fans, and everyone who had believed in her. She spoke about the importance of being true to oneself and following one's dreams, no matter how difficult the journey may be.

Billie's Impact on the Music Industry
Winning big at the Grammys wasn't just a personal victory for Billie—it was a milestone for the music industry as a whole. Billie Eilish was proof that young, innovative artists could take the industry by storm, defying conventions and creating music that mattered.
Billie's success at the Grammys was a reflection of the changing landscape of music. She represented a new wave of artists who were unapologetically themselves, who pushed boundaries, and who weren't afraid

to speak their minds. Billie's Grammy Night was a celebration of individuality, talent, and the power of music to change the world. Billie's Grammy Night was a turning point in her career, but it wasn't the end. Billie had bigger dreams and even more goals. She was already thinking about what was next—more music, more tours, and more opportunities to connect with her fans. Billie was determined to use her platform for good, to continue using her voice to inspire others. She wanted to be a role model for kids everywhere, showing them that they could achieve their dreams if they were willing to work hard and stay true to themselves.

Billie Eilish's Grammy Night was a celebration of her journey so far, but it was also just the beginning. There was so much

BILLIE EILISH…………..

more to come—more music, more milestones, and more moments that would shape her legacy in the music world.

Chapter 10: Inspiring the World: More Than Just Music

Billie Eilish isn't just a musician; she's a role model, an advocate, and a powerful voice for change. Her influence extends far beyond her Grammy-winning music. Billie uses her platform to speak out on important issues, to challenge norms, and to connect with fans in meaningful ways. She's more than just a pop star—she's a global icon who inspires millions around the world.

From the very beginning, Billie Eilish was outspoken about issues that mattered to her. She didn't want to be just another artist making music for the sake of fame and fortune. Billie wanted to make a difference, to use her influence to create positive change. Whether it's mental health awareness, environmental activism, or speaking up for underrepresented voices, Billie has always used her platform to raise awareness and start conversations.

Billie's song "All the Good Girls Go to Hell" is a prime example of her activism through music. The song addresses climate change, greed, and corporate irresponsibility. The music video, which features Billie singing in a flaming forest, captures the urgency of the message. It's a powerful visual that aligns with Billie's values and challenges fans to think critically about the world around them.

Championing Mental Health

Mental health is another cause that is close to Billie's heart. She has been open about her own struggles, sharing her experiences

BILLIE EILISH..............

to help others who might be going through similar situations. In a world where mental health issues are often stigmatized, Billie has been a strong advocate for breaking the silence and seeking help.

Billie's song "Bury a Friend" deals with themes of fear, anxiety, and self-doubt. The eerie, haunting track is a raw portrayal of Billie's inner struggles. It's a song that many listeners can relate to, and it's part of Billie's larger mission to normalize conversations about mental health. She uses her music as a tool to reach out to fans, to let them know they are not alone, and to encourage them to take care of their well-being.

Using Fashion as a Form of Self-Expression
Billie Eilish's fashion sense is as unconventional as her music. She doesn't

conform to traditional standards of beauty or fashion. Instead, she uses clothing as a form of self-expression and a way to send powerful messages. Billie's oversized clothes, baggy pants, and graphic tees are more than just a fashion statement—they are a symbol of empowerment and individuality.

At red carpet events and in her music videos, Billie often wears outfits that challenge expectations. Whether it's a baggy suit, a giant hoodie, or a custom-made gown, Billie's fashion choices are a reflection of her unique personality and her desire to stand out. She uses her wardrobe to send a message that being different is something to be celebrated, not hidden.

Creating a Safe Space for Fans

Billie Eilish's relationship with her fans is special. She's created a safe and welcoming space for people who feel misunderstood or out of place. Billie's concerts are more than just performances—they are opportunities for fans to connect, to feel understood, and to be part of a community. Billie often shares personal stories, answers questions, and engages with fans on social media, showing them that they matter.

Billie's fan base is diverse, spanning different cultures, backgrounds, and ages. She has connected with young people in a profound way, offering them a sense of belonging and hope. Billie's music and message resonate with those who feel like outsiders, and she uses her platform to remind them that they are not alone.

BILLIE EILISH..............

Billie's Influence Beyond Music

Billie Eilish's impact goes beyond music—it extends into art, activism, fashion, and more. She's not just a pop star; she's a cultural icon. Billie has inspired a generation of artists, activists, and fans to be unapologetically themselves, to question norms, and to stand up for what they believe in.

Through her lyrics, interviews, and social media presence, Billie has become a voice for change. She speaks out on issues like gender equality, mental health, and environmental sustainability. Billie's influence can be seen in the way young people express themselves today—through fashion, art, and activism.

The Future of Billie Eilish

BILLIE EILISH..............

Billie Eilish's future is bright and full of possibilities. She continues to evolve as an artist, exploring new sounds and themes in her music. Billie has hinted at new projects, collaborations, and tours, and her fans are excited to see what she has in store.

But Billie's goals go beyond music. She wants to use her platform to make a lasting impact on the world. Billie is passionate about environmental activism, and she's working on initiatives to reduce waste, promote sustainability, and raise awareness about climate change. She's also focused on mental health, using her voice to challenge the stigma and create a more supportive environment for everyone.

Billie's journey is just beginning. She's already achieved so much, but she's hungry for more. Billie Eilish is not just a pop

BILLIE EILISH…………..

star—she's a force for good, a trailblazer, and a symbol of change. Her story is one of resilience, creativity, and the power of staying true to oneself.

Chapter 11: Billie's Biggest Fans: Connecting with Kids Like You

Billie Eilish has always had a special connection with her fans. For her, music is more than just a career; it's a way to bond with people around the world. She understands the importance of creating a safe space where everyone can feel accepted and understood. Through her music, Billie reaches out to kids like you—those who might feel different, unique, or misunderstood.

A Universal Appeal
Billie's music speaks to kids of all ages and backgrounds. Whether you're into pop, rock, or indie music, there's something for everyone in Billie's discography. Her songs

cover a wide range of topics—from heartbreak and self-discovery to social issues and personal growth. Billie's lyrics are relatable and often express feelings that kids experience in their everyday lives.

Songs like "Lovely" (with Khalid) and "When the Party's Over" tackle themes of loneliness and disappointment, emotions that many kids can relate to. Billie's voice, both in her singing and songwriting, is honest and vulnerable, and it connects with fans on a deep level. She's not afraid to be herself, and that's why so many kids look up to her.

Billie's Role as an Inspiration
Billie's influence goes beyond just the music. She's become a role model for kids all over

the world. She encourages her fans to be true to themselves, to express themselves freely, and to not be afraid to stand out. Billie shows that it's okay to be different, and that's a powerful message for kids who might feel like they don't fit in.

Billie's willingness to speak out about mental health, climate change, and societal issues teaches kids that they have a voice, too. She encourages them to use it for good and to advocate for the things they care about. Billie's story is about more than just fame and fortune—she's about purpose, passion, and making a difference.

Billie has created a global community of fans who share a love for her music and a commitment to positivity. Through social media, Billie connects with her fans on a personal level. She shares updates, interacts with comments, and creates content that brings her closer to her audience. Billie's fan base is diverse, and she encourages her followers to support each other and to be kind.

Billie's concerts are a testament to the power of community. At her shows, you'll see kids of all ages, cultures, and backgrounds singing along to every word. The energy is electric, and it's clear that Billie's music brings people together. Fans often describe her concerts as transformative experiences, a chance to forget about their troubles and to just be in the moment.

The Power of Billie's Message

Billie's message is simple yet profound: be yourself, embrace who you are, and don't let anyone dim your light. Her music and lyrics serve as a reminder that it's okay to feel a wide range of emotions, from sadness to joy, and everything in between. Billie's honesty is refreshing, and it resonates with kids who might be going through similar experiences. Songs like "Xanny" and "Wish You Were Gay" tackle the complexities of relationships and self-acceptance. Billie's willingness to discuss these topics openly shows her commitment to normalizing conversations about mental health, sexuality, and identity. Her music encourages kids to think critically about the world around them and to challenge societal norms.

Inspiring Change and Challenging Norms
Billie's influence extends beyond just music—she's a change-maker. She uses her

platform to challenge norms, to question what's accepted, and to inspire others to do the same. Billie's bold fashion choices, outspoken views, and willingness to speak her mind make her a powerful role model for kids who are searching for their own identities.

Through her lyrics, Billie encourages kids to be advocates for change. Whether it's through petitions, social media campaigns, or simply starting conversations, Billie's fans are inspired to take action. Billie's music is not just entertainment—it's a call to action, a reminder that everyone has the power to make a difference.

A Lasting Impact

Billie's connection with her fans is one that will last a lifetime. She's more than just a pop star—she's a friend, a mentor, and a source of inspiration. Billie's impact goes beyond just her music; it's about the relationships she's built and the values she's instilled in her fans. Kids who look up to Billie are learning valuable lessons about authenticity, empathy, and activism.

Billie Eilish's influence will continue to grow as she evolves as an artist and an advocate. Her story is one of resilience, creativity, and the power of staying true to oneself. Billie's biggest fans are not just fans—they are a community, a family, and a movement. And they have Billie Eilish to thank for bringing them together.

Chapter 12: What's Next for Billie?

As Billie Eilish continues to grow as an artist, there's always something exciting on the horizon. Billie's journey is far from over, and she has big dreams and plans for the future. From new music to innovative projects, there's a lot to look forward to for Billie and her fans. Let's dive into what's next for Billie Eilish!

A New Era of Music
Billie's music is ever-evolving. With each album, she pushes boundaries, experiments with new sounds, and challenges herself creatively. Fans can expect even more of Billie's signature style: haunting melodies, introspective lyrics, and a mix of genres that keep everyone guessing. Billie's sophomore

album, "Happier Than Ever", was a testament to her growth as an artist, showcasing her versatility and lyrical depth. And the best part? There's more to come! Billie has already hinted at what's next. She's been working on new projects, including possible collaborations with other artists. Billie's openness to collaboration shows her willingness to continue learning and growing as a musician. Whether it's teaming up with pop stars or indie artists, Billie's music is sure to surprise and delight her fans.

Venturing Beyond Music
Billie is not just focused on her music career; she's also exploring other creative avenues. She's interested in fashion, film, and even acting. Billie's unique sense of

style has already made waves in the fashion industry. She's collaborated with major brands and launched her own merchandise lines. Billie's fashion choices are bold, experimental, and a reflection of her individuality.

There are rumors that Billie might make her acting debut in the near future. Whether it's a role in a film, a TV series, or even a music video, Billie's fans are excited to see her on screen. Billie's acting skills could provide a new dimension to her creative expression and expand her influence even further.

Activism and Advocacy

Billie has always used her platform to speak out on important issues. From climate change to mental health, Billie's voice is one that carries weight. She's passionate about making a difference and inspiring others to do the same. Billie's fans look up to her not just for her music but for her courage and integrity.

Expect Billie to continue advocating for causes she believes in. She's already involved in various environmental initiatives and social justice campaigns. Billie's goal is to empower her fans to take action and become agents of change in their own communities. Whether it's through social media, charity events, or grassroots movements, Billie's influence is set to inspire a new generation of activists.

Touring the World

One of the most exciting things for fans is the prospect of seeing Billie live in concert. Billie's tours are known for their high energy, engaging performances, and memorable moments. With her unique stage presence and passionate delivery, Billie creates an atmosphere that's both intimate and electrifying.

Billie's last tour, "Where Do We Go?", was a huge success. It sold out arenas worldwide and featured stunning visuals, choreographed dances, and, of course, live music. Billie's stage shows are a visual and auditory experience that leaves fans in awe. And with new music on the way, fans can expect an even bigger and better show next time around.

Exploring New Creative Frontiers

Billie is not content with staying in one lane. She's always looking for new ways to express herself and push creative boundaries.

Billie's curiosity and willingness to experiment have been a driving force in her career. From directing music videos to designing stage outfits, Billie is involved in every aspect of her creative process.

There are whispers about Billie starting her own production company or even launching a podcast. Billie's voice is one that needs to be heard, and she's always looking for new ways to share her thoughts and ideas with the world. Whether it's through music, film, or other media, Billie's goal is to create art that resonates and makes a difference.

Personal Growth and Development
Billie Eilish is constantly evolving as a person. As she navigates the ups and downs of fame, Billie remains grounded and focused on her values. She's learned a lot

over the years, and she's not afraid to share her experiences with her fans. Billie's journey is a testament to the power of growth and self-discovery.

In the future, Billie aims to continue exploring new aspects of herself, both personally and professionally. She's been candid about her struggles with mental health and her journey towards self-acceptance. Billie's openness is inspiring and helps break down the stigma around these important topics.

Looking Ahead

The future is bright for Billie Eilish. With a clear sense of direction and a strong vision for her career, Billie is set to make an even bigger impact in the years to come. Whether it's through her music, activism, fashion, or other creative pursuits, Billie's goal is to leave a lasting legacy. Billie Eilish is more than just a pop star; she's a cultural force, a beacon of change, and an inspiration for kids around the world.

As Billie continues to grow, she remains dedicated to her fans. Her commitment to authenticity, creativity, and social responsibility is what makes her an enduring and beloved figure. Billie's story is one of perseverance, passion, and the courage to be true to oneself.

Chapter 13: Lessons from Billie: Dare to Be Different

Billie Eilish is not your average pop star. From her music to her fashion sense, Billie has always marched to the beat of her own drum. But what really sets her apart is her fearless approach to being herself. In a world where conformity often reigns, Billie's journey is a powerful reminder that it's okay—and even empowering—to be different. Let's explore the lessons kids can learn from Billie's inspiring journey.

Embrace Your Uniqueness
One of the most valuable lessons Billie teaches is the importance of embracing who you are, even if it's not what's expected or "cool." Billie didn't fit into the typical pop

star mold, and she didn't try to. Instead, she carved out her own space in the music industry with her distinct style and sound. Whether it's her baggy clothes, neon hair, or lyrics that speak to deep emotions, Billie is unapologetically herself. She encourages kids to be true to their own interests, passions, and quirks.

Be Fearless in Pursuing Your Passions
Billie's success didn't come overnight. She had to work hard, face challenges, and take risks along the way. From writing her first song in her bedroom to releasing her first album, Billie was fearless in pursuing her passion for music. She didn't let anyone tell her what she could or couldn't do. Billie shows kids that it's important to go after what you love, even if it means stepping

outside your comfort zone. Fear is a natural part of trying new things, but it's also an opportunity for growth and learning.

Stay True to Your Artistic Vision

Billie's music is a reflection of her artistic vision. She's involved in every aspect of her work, from songwriting to music videos, to ensure that her message is authentic. Billie doesn't compromise her vision just to please others. This commitment to staying true to herself is a valuable lesson for kids. It teaches them the importance of believing in their own creative ideas and not letting outside pressures dictate their choices.

Learn from Mistakes and Move Forward

No one is perfect, and Billie is no exception. She's faced criticism, controversy, and tough times, but she's always handled them with grace and resilience. Billie teaches kids that mistakes are a natural part of life, and they don't define you. What matters is how you learn from them and move forward. Billie's ability to bounce back from setbacks is inspiring. She shows that it's possible to take negative experiences and turn them into something positive.

Connect with Others through Your Voice
Billie's music isn't just about her. It's about connecting with her audience and creating a sense of community. Billie's lyrics often reflect universal emotions, struggles, and dreams. She uses her platform to address important issues like mental health, self-acceptance, and social justice. Billie's message is clear: we're all in this together.

She encourages kids to use their own voices to speak up for what they believe in and to be kind, empathetic, and supportive of others.

Practice Self-Care
Billie is open about her struggles with mental health and the importance of self-care. She doesn't shy away from discussing topics that are often stigmatized. Billie's transparency is a reminder that it's okay to not be okay sometimes. She encourages kids to take care of their mental and emotional well-being, whether it's through talking to someone they trust, doing something they love, or simply taking time for themselves. Billie's own journey has shown her the value of prioritizing self-care,

and she shares these lessons to help others do the same.

Celebrate Diversity

Billie's message is all about inclusivity and celebrating diversity. She's known for breaking down barriers and challenging norms. Billie embraces people from all walks of life and celebrates their differences. This inclusive spirit is something kids can learn from and emulate in their own lives. Whether it's respecting others' opinions, understanding different cultures, or appreciating various forms of art, Billie encourages kids to be open-minded and accepting of all people.

Dare to Dream Big

Billie's success is proof that big dreams can come true. She started with a small bedroom studio and turned it into a global career. Billie teaches kids that their dreams are within reach if they're willing to work for them. She shows that it's important to think big, set goals, and never give up on achieving them. Billie's journey from a young girl with big dreams to a Grammy-winning artist is a story of determination and perseverance that kids can find incredibly inspiring.

Take Action
Billie's activism is an extension of her values and beliefs. She uses her platform to make a difference and encourage others to do the same. Billie teaches kids that it's not enough to just talk about what's wrong in the world;

you have to take action to make things right. Whether it's participating in environmental campaigns, supporting charities, or simply speaking out on social media, Billie shows that small actions can lead to big changes.

Be Inspired, Not Imitated
Billie encourages kids to be inspired by her journey but also to find their own paths. She's not interested in clones or followers; she wants kids to create their own stories. Billie's journey is unique, and she wants kids to carve out their own paths, too. She reminds them that they have the power to shape their own futures. Billie's story is not just about fame and success; it's about individuality, resilience, and the courage to be different.

Chapter 14: A Legacy of Inspiration and Empowerment

As we wrap up this biography of Billie Eilish, it's clear that her journey is much more than just a tale of fame and fortune. Billie's story is a powerful testament to the impact one individual can have when they embrace their true self and pursue their passions with determination and integrity. From a young girl making music in her bedroom to a global superstar who breaks records and inspires millions, Billie's life is a beacon of hope and empowerment. In this final chapter, let's reflect on the key takeaways from her journey and explore how Billie's legacy continues to inspire and shape the world.

BILLIE EILISH..............

A Beacon of Authenticity

Billie's journey to success is built on authenticity. From her distinctive style to her honest lyrics, Billie has always been true to herself. She didn't conform to industry norms or chase after a cookie-cutter image. Instead, Billie set her own rules and defined her own brand of stardom. Her willingness to be different and unapologetically herself has resonated with fans around the world. Billie's story shows that authenticity is a powerful tool for connecting with people and creating meaningful art.

Championing Self-Expression

Billie's music and fashion choices have always been a form of self-expression. She uses her voice to tell her story, share her experiences, and explore a wide range of emotions. Billie's fearless approach to creativity teaches kids that it's okay to express themselves in whatever way feels right to them. Whether it's through writing, painting, dancing, or any other form of creative outlet, Billie encourages kids to embrace their individuality and let their voices be heard.

Breaking Barriers and Challenging Norms

Billie's impact goes beyond music. She's a voice for change, using her platform to address important issues like mental health, climate change, and social justice. Billie's ability to speak out on these topics and challenge the status quo is a testament to her strength and courage. She's not afraid to stand up for what she believes in, even if it means going against the grain. Billie's journey is a reminder that it's important to question authority, challenge norms, and push for positive change in the world.

Inspiring Future Generations

Billie's story is an inspiration for kids around the globe. She's shown that you don't have to follow a traditional path to achieve your dreams. Billie's success is proof that hard work, creativity, and a willingness to be different can lead to greatness. She's empowered kids to believe in themselves and their abilities, no matter how unconventional they may seem. Billie's legacy is one of empowerment—she's shown that anyone can achieve their goals if they dare to be different and stay true to themselves.

A Call to Action

Billie's impact goes beyond the music industry. She's a role model who encourages kids to use their voices for good. Billie's story is a call to action for kids to get involved in their communities, stand up for what they believe in, and make a positive impact on the world. She teaches them that even small actions can lead to big changes. Whether it's speaking out on social media, joining environmental campaigns, or supporting social justice causes, Billie's legacy is about taking responsibility and making a difference.

BILLIE EILISH..............

The Future of Billie Eilish

As Billie continues to evolve as an artist, her impact on the world will only grow stronger. She's already accomplished so much, but Billie's story is far from over. Her journey is a reminder that fame is not the ultimate goal; rather, it's about using your platform to create a lasting legacy. Billie's future plans include new music, more activism, and continuing to inspire the next generation. Billie's legacy will be one of inspiration, creativity, and empowerment—a beacon for kids everywhere to follow their own paths and make a difference in the world.

The Power of Being Different

BILLIE EILISH…………..

Billie's legacy is not just about her music or her awards; it's about the values she stands for. Billie's journey is a reminder that being different is a strength, not a weakness. She's shown kids that they have the power to shape their own futures, challenge the status quo, and create change in the world. Billie's story is about embracing individuality, taking risks, and following one's passions without fear of judgment or failure. Her journey is a testament to the idea that being different can lead to greatness.

A Message of Hope

Billie's story is one of hope and possibility. She's shown that no matter where you come from or what challenges you face, you can achieve greatness if you stay true to yourself and keep pushing forward. Billie's journey is a reminder that we all have the power to create our own futures and leave a positive mark on the world. Billie's legacy is a beacon of inspiration, showing kids that they are capable of achieving their dreams and making a difference, just like she has.

A Lasting Impact

As we conclude this biography of Billie Eilish, it's clear that her story is much more than just a celebrity tale. Billie's journey is a legacy of inspiration, creativity, and empowerment. She's shown kids that they have the power to be different, to challenge norms, and to change the world for the better. Billie's story is a reminder that it's

BILLIE EILISH…………..

okay to be unique, to take risks, and to dream big. Billie's legacy will live on through her music, her activism, and the countless kids who are inspired by her journey.

BILLIE EILISH..............

Fun facts about Billie Eilish:

1. Multi-talented Family: Billie comes from a very musical family. Both her parents are actors and musicians. Her mother, Maggie Baird, is also a screenwriter, and her father, Patrick O'Connell, is an actor who performs in comedy plays.

2. Name Meaning: Billie's full name is Billie Eilish Pirate Baird O'Connell. Her middle name, Pirate, was inspired by a character in a movie her parents liked.

3. Early Music Inspiration: Billie grew up listening to a wide variety of music, including classics from The Beatles, Nirvana, and Radiohead. These artists have greatly influenced her sound and style.

4. Home Recording Studio: She and her older brother, Finneas, started recording songs in their family's basement studio when Billie was just 11 years old. They used basic equipment and the space to create her early music.

5. Breakout Hit: Her single "Ocean Eyes," which she wrote when she was just 13 years old, became a viral hit and catapulted her to fame. It was originally intended to be a track for her dance class.

6. Creative Wardrobe: Billie is known for her unique fashion style. She often wears oversized clothes and layers them to make a statement about body positivity and comfort over trends. Her baggy clothing helps her

stay away from body-shaming from the media.

7. Green Hair: Billie's distinctive green hair, which she debuted in 2019, became a signature look. The color change was both a style choice and a reflection of her mood at the time, as she wanted to show her playful and carefree side.

8. Environmental Activist: Billie is an outspoken advocate for climate change and environmental issues. She has urged her fans to reduce their carbon footprint and take better care of the planet. She's even partnered with Greenpeace for campaigns promoting sustainable living.

9. First Grammy: At just 18 years old, Billie became the youngest artist ever to win the prestigious Grammy Award for Album of the Year in 2020 for her debut album "When We All Fall Asleep, Where Do We Go?".

10. Social Media Star: Billie's Instagram account has millions of followers. She uses her platform not only to share her music but also to connect with her fans and raise awareness on various social issues.

11. Health Challenges: Billie has struggled with Tourette Syndrome since she was a child, but she doesn't let it define her. She has been very open about her experience, using her platform to raise awareness and support others who also live with the condition.

BILLIE EILISH..............

12. Loves Animals: Billie is a big animal lover and has multiple pets, including a pit bull named Shark, a cat named Mishy, and a snake named Pepper. She's also a vegetarian, aligning with her views on environmental sustainability.

13. No Private Jet: Unlike many of her celebrity peers, Billie does not use a private jet. She's committed to reducing her carbon footprint and prefers commercial flights when traveling.

14. Big on Video Games: Billie is a huge fan of video games, especially "The Legend of Zelda" series. She even has a gaming setup in her tour bus so she can play during downtime.

BILLIE EILISH…………...

15. Youth Advocate: Billie often talks about the importance of youth activism and encourages kids to get involved in causes they care about. She believes young people have the power to change the world.

BILLIE EILISH…………..

Trivia questions

Kids! Let's see how well you know Billie Eilish

1. What is Billie Eilish's full birth name?

A) Billie Eilish Pirate Baird O'Connell

B) Billie Eilish Finneas O'Connell

C) Billie Pirate Baird Eilish

D) Billie Baird Finneas O'Connell

BILLIE EILISH…………..

2. At what age did Billie Eilish first gain widespread recognition with her song "Ocean Eyes"?

A) 12 years old

B) 13 years old

C) 14 years old

D) 15 years old

3. Who helped Billie Eilish write and produce most of her early music?

A) Her sister

BILLIE EILISH..............

B) Her mother

C) Her brother, Finneas O'Connell

D) A professional producer

4. Which Grammy category did Billie Eilish win at the 2020 Grammy Awards?

A) Best New Artist

B) Record of the Year

C) Song of the Year

D) Album of the Year

BILLIE EILISH…………..

5. What color is Billie Eilish's hair known to be dyed?

A) Blue

B) Green

C) Pink

D) Purple

6. Billie Eilish has been open about living with what condition?

A) Autism

BILLIE EILISH..............

B) ADHD

C) Tourette Syndrome

D) Anxiety Disorder

7. What song was Billie Eilish's first major single that brought her to viral fame?

A) "Bad Guy"

B) "Bury a Friend"

C) "Everything I Wanted"

D) "Ocean Eyes"

BILLIE EILISH…………..

8. Which video game series does Billie Eilish frequently mention as one of her favorites?

A) Mario Kart

B) The Legend of Zelda

C) Minecraft

D) Pokemon

9. Billie Eilish made history at the Grammy Awards by being the youngest artist ever to win which prestigious award?

BILLIE EILISH..............

A) Best New Artist

B) Record of the Year

C) Album of the Year

D) Song of the Year

10. Why does Billie Eilish prefer not to use private jets?

A) For comfort

B) To reduce her carbon footprint

C) To avoid delays

BILLIE EILISH..............

D) She prefers to travel by train

11. What type of pet does Billie Eilish have named Shark?

A) A cat

B) A pit bull

C) A rabbit

D) A parrot

12. Besides Instagram, which other social media platform does Billie use to connect with fans?

A) Snapchat

B) TikTok

C) Twitter

D) Facebook

13. What environmental cause is Billie Eilish most vocal about advocating for?

A) Ocean pollution

BILLIE EILISH…………..

B) Deforestation

C) Climate change

D) Animal rights

14. In what year did Billie Eilish release her debut album?

A) 2017

B) 2018

C) 2019

D) 2020

BILLIE EILISH…………..

15. Which major music festival did Billie Eilish perform at in 2019, significantly boosting her fame?

A) Bonnaroo

B) Coachella

C) Lollapalooza

D) Glastonbury

16. What was Billie's reaction to winning her first Grammy for Album of the Year?

BILLIE EILISH..............

A) She cried tears of joy.

B) She thanked her family and fans.

C) She was speechless and in shock.

D) She danced with excitement.

17. What was the inspiration behind Billie's choice of green hair color?

A) To stand out

B) To match her album cover

C) To reflect her mood

BILLIE EILISH..............

D) To go with her favorite outfit

18. Besides her music, in what other area does Billie Eilish use her platform to speak out?

A) Fashion

B) Mental health

C) Sports

D) Cooking

BILLIE EILISH…………..

19. How does Billie describe her unique fashion style?

A) Vintage chic

B) Minimalist

C) Oversized and comfortable

D) Glamorous

20. What year did Billie Eilish sign with Interscope Records?

A) 2014

B) 2015

BILLIE EILISH..............

C) 2016

D) 2017

Answers

1. What is Billie Eilish's full birth name?
A: Billie Eilish Pirate Baird O'Connell

2. At what age did Billie Eilish first gain widespread recognition with her song "Ocean Eyes"?
B: 13 years old

3. Who helped Billie Eilish write and produce most of her early music?
C: Her brother, Finneas O'Connell

BILLIE EILISH...............

4. Which Grammy category did Billie Eilish win at the 2020 Grammy Awards?
D: Album of the Year

5. What color is Billie Eilish's hair known to be dyed?
B: Green

6. Billie Eilish has been open about living with what condition?
C: Tourette Syndrome

7. What song was Billie Eilish's first major single that brought her to viral fame?
D: "Ocean Eyes"

8. Which video game series does Billie Eilish frequently mention as one of her favorites?

127

BILLIE EILISH..............

B: The Legend of Zelda

9. Billie Eilish made history at the Grammy Awards by being the youngest artist ever to win which prestigious award?
C: Album of the Year

10. Why does Billie Eilish prefer not to use private jets?
B: To reduce her carbon footprint.

11. What type of pet does Billie Eilish have named Shark?
B: A pit bull

12. Besides Instagram, which other social media platform does Billie use to connect with fans?
B: TikTok

BILLIE EILISH..............

13. What environmental cause is Billie Eilish most vocal about advocating for?
C: Climate change

14. In what year did Billie Eilish release her debut album?
C: 2019

15. Which major music festival did Billie Eilish perform at in 2019, significantly boosting her fame?
B: Coachella

16. What was Billie's reaction to winning her first Grammy for Album of the Year?
C: She was speechless and in shock.

BILLIE EILISH..............

17. What was the inspiration behind Billie's choice of green hair color?
C: To reflect her mood.

18. Besides her music, in what other area does Billie Eilish use her platform to speak out?
B: Mental health

19. How does Billie describe her unique fashion style?
C: Oversized and comfortable

20. What year did Billie Eilish sign with Interscope Records?
B: 2015

Conclusion

Billie Eilish's journey from a young girl singing family songs to becoming a global superstar with Grammy wins and a voice that resonates with millions is a testament to the power of creativity, resilience, and staying true to oneself. Her story is more than just fame and awards; it's about embracing uniqueness, facing challenges head-on, and using her platform to inspire and make a positive impact on the world. Billie's music isn't just catchy tunes; it's a reflection of her thoughts, emotions, and the world around her. As kids who admire Billie's journey, they can learn the importance of being themselves, following their passions, and never giving up on their dreams. Billie Eilish's story is a reminder

BILLIE EILISH..............

that we all have the power to create, dream big, and achieve greatness, no matter where we start. Her legacy is not just in her music but in the hearts and minds of her fans, encouraging them to be brave, creative, and unapologetically themselves.

Made in United States
Cleveland, OH
28 January 2025

13850233R00075